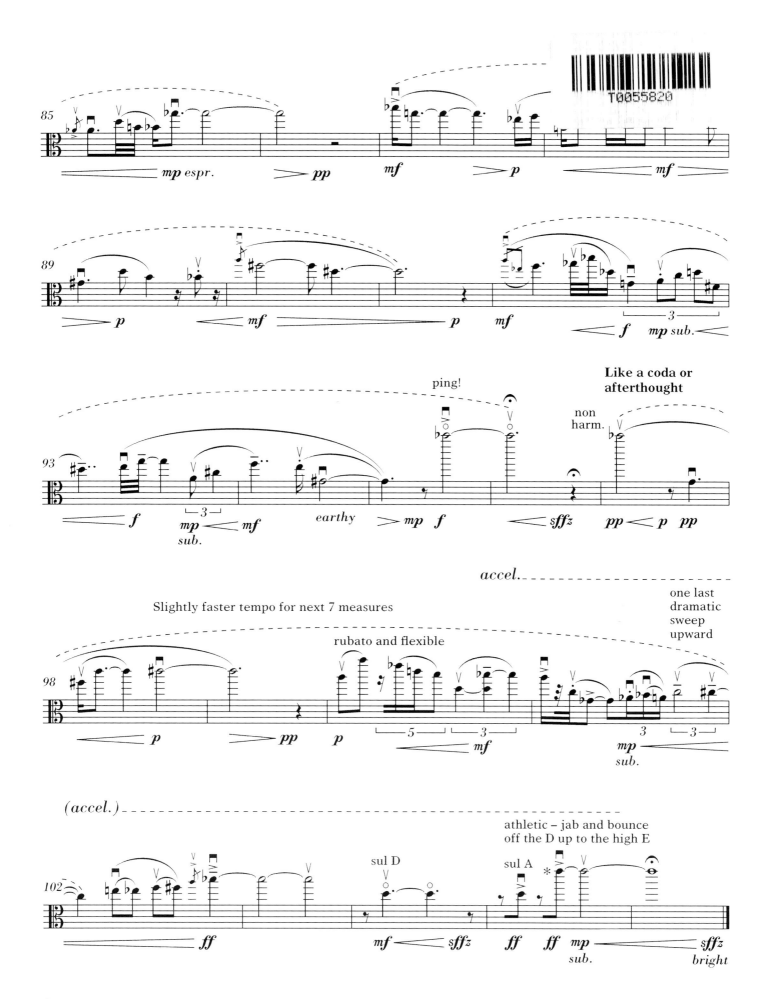

*The final note should feel naturally "in" the bow and should not be counted. Simply go with the bow and the phrase: Molto rubato.

floating

ff elegant mp p espr.

mf mp playful f ff espr. p< sub.

sul A rit. - - - - - - - - - - **Graceful** ♩ = 60

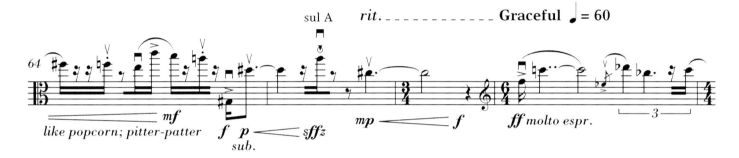

mf
like popcorn; pitter-patter f p §ffz sub. mp f ff molto espr.

mf p mf ff pp as if floating out in a distant place p back to earth again

This final phrase of DREAM CATCHER is dedicated with admiration and gratitude to Laurie Shulman on April 27, 2008 for her gala reception scrapbook.

Molto rubato sempre ♩ = 66

accel. - - - - - - - - - **Dreamy, floating and seductive – almost as if you are casting a spell**

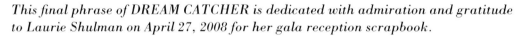

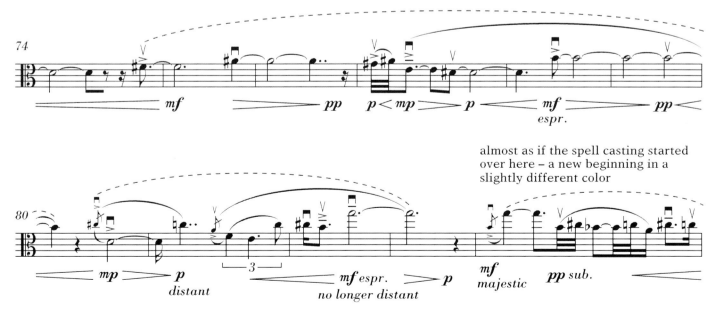

mf pp p< mp > p mf espr. pp

almost as if the spell casting started over here – a new beginning in a slightly different color

mp p distant 3 mf espr. no longer distant p mf majestic pp sub.

*Very gradually the tempo indications will keep accelerating, creating a very long-reaching, accelerating phrase.

Dream Catcher was written for and is dedicated to Maria Schleuning who gave its premiere performance on a program by "Voices of Change" 3 May 2009, in Dallas Texas.

G. SCHIRMER, Inc.

DISTRIBUTED BY

HAL•LEONARD®

ISBN 978-1-4803-4537-9

9 781480 345379